W9-AUD-898

$ 24.00

847

04/2014

SCUBA
Man

Jacques Cousteau and His Amazing Underwater Invention

Carmen Bredeson

Enslow Elementary
an imprint of
Enslow Publishers, Inc.
40 Industrial Road
Box 398
Berkeley Heights, NJ 07922
USA
http://www.enslow.com

Enslow Elementary, an imprint of Enslow Publishers, Inc.

Enslow Elementary® is a registered trademark of Enslow Publishers, Inc.

Library of Congress Cataloging-in-Publication Data

Bredeson, Carmen.
 Scuba man: Jacques Cousteau and his amazing underwater invention / Carmen Bredeson.
   p. cm. — (Inventors at work!)
 Includes index.
 Summary: "Read about Jacques Cousteau's life and the invention of the Aqua-Lung"—Provided by publisher.
 ISBN 978-0-7660-4231-5
 1. Cousteau, Jacques, 1910–1997. 2. Oceanographers—France—Biography. 3. Inventors—France—Biography.
   4. Scuba apparatus—Design and construction. I. Title.
 GC30.C68B74 2014
 688.7'6—dc23
                                    2012041456

Future editions:
Paperback ISBN: 978-1-4644-0405-4
EPUB ISBN: 978-1-4645-1222-3
Single-User PDF ISBN: 978-1-4646-1222-0
Multi-User PDF ISBN: 978-0-7660-5854-5

Printed in the United States of America

102013 Lake Book Manufacturing, Inc., Melrose Park, IL

10 9 8 7 6 5 4 3 2 1

This book has not been authorized by Jacques Cousteau or his successors.

Photo Credits: AGIP - Rue des Archives/The Granger Collection, p. 1 (Cousteau); © Albert Harlingue/Roger-Viollet/The Image Works, p. 12; AP Images/Bettmann/Corbis, p. 35; AP Images/Kathy Willens, p. 44; Bernard Laire, Frédéric Dumas International Diving Museum, p. 24; Everett Collection, pp. 4, 34, 37; The Illustrated London News, February 6, 1873, front cover, p. 21; Jacques and Simone Cousteau, p. 32; Keystone-France/Getty Images, p. 18; Library of Congress Prints and Photographs, p. 19; © National Media Museum/Science & Society Picture Library, p. 9; NOAA, p. 6; Robert B. Goodman/National Geographic Stock, p. 28; Rue des Archives/The Granger Collection, New York, p. 38; Shutterstock.com, pp. 1 (fish, goggles, diver's body), 8, 15, 22, 30, 40, 41, 42, 43; United States Patent Office, p. 25.

Cover Credit: AGIP - Rue des Archives/The Granger Collection (Cousteau); Shutterstock.com (others).

CONTENTS

Jacques Cousteau figured out a way to swim underwater with a tank of air on his back.

The Aqua-Lung Arrives!

Jacques Cousteau carried the wooden box into the house. His wife and two friends were waiting for him. They had all been waiting for this moment. Cousteau pried open the box, sent by Emile Gagnan. Inside was an Aqua-Lung!

What Is an Aqua-Lung?

Jacques Cousteau had a dream. He wanted to be able to swim with the fish. Until the 1940s, divers breathed through a long hose connected to a ship on the surface. The diver could go only as far as the hose would reach.

Inside the box was a tank that a diver could carry on his back. Then the person could swim freely underwater. It was a wonderful invention, but would it work?

Diving Bell

A diving bell had an open bottom. The bell was lowered into the water on a cable. People sat inside the bell, usually in their regular clothes. Try turning over a glass in a sink of water. Push the glass straight down. The glass does not fill up with water. A bubble of air stays in the glass. The diving bell worked the same way. People inside breathed the air in the bubble. Today, modern diving bells are used for many different kinds of underwater work.

diving bell

Learning to Swim

Jacques-Yves Cousteau was born on June 11, 1910 in France. When he was a boy, he had a disease that gave him a lot of stomachaches. He didn't eat much, so he was small and weak. Jacques couldn't run and play. He needed an exercise to make him stronger. How about swimming? It was easy to paddle in the water. Jacques learned to swim. His body got stronger.

The Cousteau family moved to New York City when Jacques was ten. One summer he went to camp in Vermont. The boys went hiking and swimming. They rode horses. Jacques didn't like horses. On his first ride, the horse threw him. The teacher told him to get back on the horse. Jacques said no.

Jacques was punished for saying no. He was sent to clean out the pond where the boys swam. There were dead tree branches in the water. This wasn't punishment! He loved being in the water. Jacques dove again and again. He had to open his eyes to see the branches. This was the first time Jacques opened his eyes underwater.

For some boys, like Jacques, swimming is the perfect activity.

How Does It Work?

Along with swimming, Jacques liked to see how things worked. He saved his allowance and bought a movie camera. The camera went everywhere with Jacques. He filmed his friends. He filmed dogs and cats. Jacques and his friends made up little plays to perform. He filmed those too. He also took the camera apart many times to clean it. He learned how it worked.

When he was twelve, Jacques decided to build a crane. He ordered plans from a magazine. The plans were for a full-size crane. A huge crane was impossible for him to build. He made

This movie camera is like the one that Jacques used as a boy. He loved making movies!

a small model instead. The crane he built was as tall as he was. It had pulleys and cranks. It could turn around, forward, and backward. It was a big job, but he did it!

Jacques loved machines and swimming. School was another matter. He didn't like to study and his grades showed it. One day his mother took his camera away because of his bad grades. Soon after, Jacques broke several windows at school. The principal suspended him for a week.

Mr. and Mrs. Cousteau wondered what to do. They decided to send Jacques to a boarding school in France. Maybe he would learn to behave. The school was very strict. There were many rules for the boys to follow. What a surprise! Jacques liked the school and obeyed the rules. He also liked his classes and studied hard. Jacques did very well at the school. He graduated in 1929 as one of the top students in his class.

After Graduation

Jacques' good grades at boarding school got him into the French Naval Academy. He graduated in 1933 as an officer in the French Navy. For the next two years, Jacques served on a ship. He sailed all over the world. He took his cameras along. He made many movies of the Navy training exercises at sea. The ship came back to France in 1935.

Jacques also wanted to fly. He learned to fly planes with the French Aviation Corps. The student pilots often staged pretend fights in the air. Jacques was there, filming with his camera. He liked the adventure of flying, but his training was cut short.

Jacques Cousteau went to the French Naval Academy.

A Terrible Accident

One night, Jacques was driving on a curvy road. Somehow he lost control of his car and it skidded off the road. The car rolled several times and crashed into a ditch. Jacques was hurt very badly. It was two o'clock in the morning. There were no cars going by. Jacques pulled himself out of the wrecked car. He stumbled and crawled along the road. After a few miles, he found a house and some help.

Jacques was taken to the hospital. Both of his arms were broken. His right arm was very bad. Most of the bones were broken. There was also a bad infection in the arm. The doctors wanted to take off his arm right away. They thought the infection would spread. It might kill Jacques. He refused to have his arm amputated. He said, "I would rather die than live a life without both my arms."

The infection did not kill him. Both of his arms healed, but his right arm was useless. He couldn't even move his fingers. For eight months, he did painful exercises. They didn't help much either. After all that time, he could move only a couple of fingers.

Swimming Helps Again

The hospital had done all it could. Cousteau was transferred to a Navy base near the sea. He looked at the sea and remembered swimming as a boy. It had made him stronger and healthier. Maybe swimming would be good for his useless arm. Cousteau started swimming every day.

Soon he could move his arm a little and then a little more. Before long he was swimming with both of his arms. His right arm would always be weak, but he could use it again. Flight school was finished for Jacques Cousteau. He needed two good arms to fly a plane. But there were other jobs in the Navy for him, so he stayed on active duty.

During this time, Cousteau went to a dance in town. He met a young woman named Simone Melchoir. They fell in love and were married a few months later. In the years ahead, they would have two sons, Jean-Michel and Philippe. Simone was the daughter of a Navy Admiral. She also loved the sea and swimming.

Simone shared Jacque's love of swimming and the sea.

Eyes on the Sea

Jacques Cousteau had a very good friend in the Navy. He was Lieutenant Philippe Tailliez. One day they went to the beach. Cousteau borrowed a pair of goggles from his friend. Cousteau had never looked through goggles before. He was amazed! He saw rocks covered with colorful algae. Beautiful fish swam before his eyes. Jacques Cousteau's life changed. He said: "It happened to me on that summer's day, when my eyes were opened on the sea." He wanted to see what was in the ocean. He wanted to explore the bottom of the sea. He wanted to swim like a fish.

A New Way to Dive

In the late 1930s, Cousteau met Frédéric Dumas at the beach. Dumas was a local spear fisherman. He could hold his breath for three minutes as he dove for fish. He also knew how to make a snorkel. He taught Cousteau how to make a breathing tube from a garden hose. Now Cousteau could look into the water for as long as he liked. But he still could not dive into deep water.

At that time, diving equipment was big and bulky. Divers wore metal helmets, big diving suits, and boots. The diver was attached by a hose to a boat overhead. The boat had an air pump. Air was pumped down to the suit and helmet. Extra air bubbled out of a valve on the top of the helmet. The diver could not swim or move

17

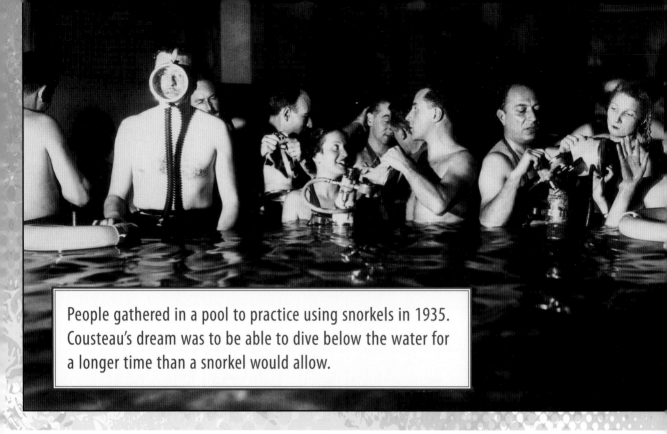

People gathered in a pool to practice using snorkels in 1935. Cousteau's dream was to be able to dive below the water for a longer time than a snorkel would allow.

around very much. Cousteau tried a diving suit one time. He didn't like it. He wanted to swim freely underwater. A diver would have to carry a supply of air to do that.

One of the men on Cousteau's Navy ship built an air tank. He filled the tank with pure oxygen. He connected the tank to a mask with a piece of bike inner tube. Cousteau tried it out in the ocean. There were two men above in a small boat. They watched in case anything went wrong.

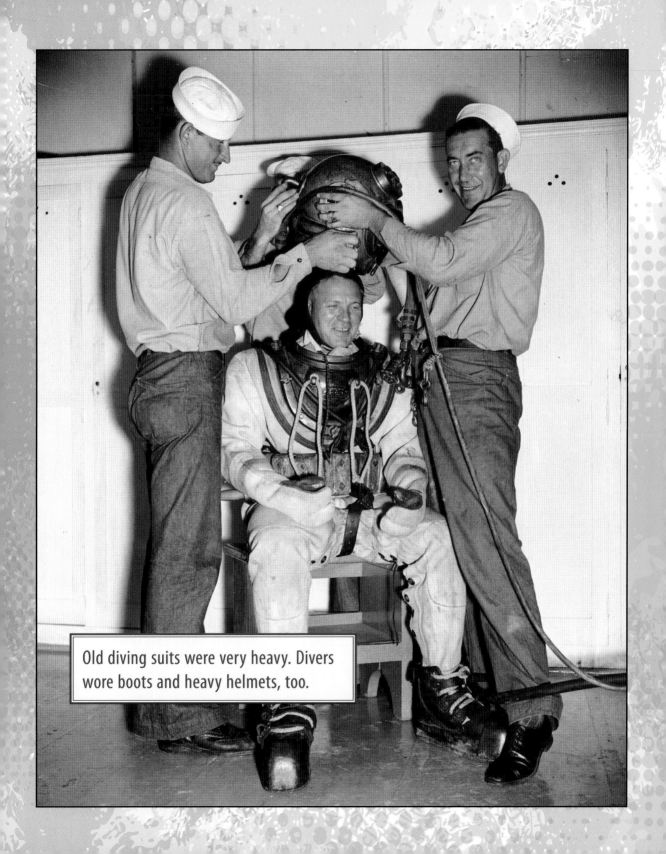

Old diving suits were very heavy. Divers wore boots and heavy helmets, too.

Almost the End

At first the air tank seemed to work fine. Cousteau could breathe easily. A beautiful fish swam by. He followed it deeper and deeper. Suddenly Cousteau's legs started to shake. Then his back bent into a bow shape. He ripped off his weight belt and then passed out. Cousteau's body floated to the surface. The men pulled him into the boat and brought him around. Cousteau never tried to dive with pure oxygen again.

Pure oxygen in the tank is what nearly killed Jacques Cousteau. Water is very heavy. The deeper a diver goes, the more pressure there is on his body. Extra pressure forces too much oxygen into the blood. That extra oxygen caused Cousteau to have a seizure.

The air we breathe is made of 78 percent nitrogen, 21 percent oxygen, and 1 percent other gases. That is the safe mixture of gases for divers to breathe. Jacques Cousteau learned this lesson the hard way.

Many people did not like to dive in heavy diving suits. Cousteau wanted to be able to swim freely without such heavy equipment.

Too Much Pressure

Finding the right mix of air was not the only problem to solve. The weight of the water on top of a diver squashes his lungs. The pressure in them builds up. If there is too much pressure, the lungs can burst. Cousteau wanted an air tank that could make the pressure in the lungs and the pressure of the water equal. The tank needed a regulator to do this.

real fact!

Diving Hard Hat

Augustus Siebe invented the diving hard hat in 1819. It was a helmet made of metal with a hose attached. Air was pumped down the hose to the helmet. Heavy weights kept the diver in place on the ocean floor.

In December 1942, Cousteau met an engineer named Emile Gagnan. He asked if Gagnan could develop a regulator to work with a tank of air. Cousteau believed that a regulator was the key to diving. Gagnan had some experience with regulators already. He had designed a regulator to work with a car engine. Instead of running on gasoline, the engine ran on natural gas using his new regulator.

Emile Gagnan and Cousteau went to work. They designed a regulator that was about the size of a fist. It sat on top of the air tank. There was a rubber disc in the middle of the regulator. One side of the disc would be open to the water. The other side would face into the tank of air. The disc was joined to an air supply valve in the regulator.

The regulator was supposed to work like this: As the diver went deeper, the water pressed down harder. Water also pressed on the rubber disc. Then the disc bent inward. This caused the valve to open wider,

This is the regulator that Cousteau invented. It is now in a museum.

putting more air into the hoses. The extra air then pressed back on the disc.

As the diver came back up, there was less water pressure. Then the rubber disc bent outward. That made the air supply valve close a little. Less air went into the hoses. The diver went up and down. The regulator kept the water pressure and air pressure the same.

The diving gear was finally ready. Cousteau tried it out in a river. It worked as long as he was upright. When he was upside down, the air stopped. He could

A New Way to Dive

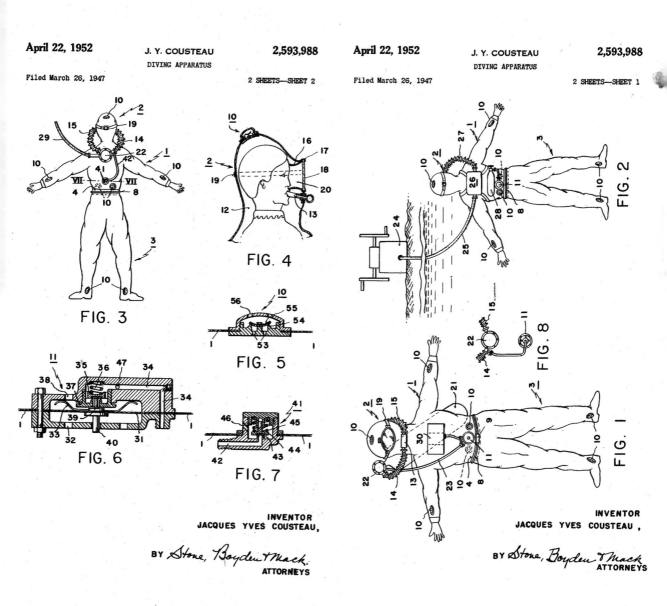

April 22, 1952   J. Y. COUSTEAU   2,593,988
DIVING APPARATUS
Filed March 26, 1947   2 SHEETS—SHEET 2

FIG. 3

FIG. 4

FIG. 5

FIG. 6

FIG. 7

April 22, 1952   J. Y. COUSTEAU   2,593,988
DIVING APPARATUS
Filed March 26, 1947   2 SHEETS—SHEET 1

FIG. 2

FIG. 8

FIG. 1

INVENTOR
JACQUES YVES COUSTEAU,
BY Stone, Boyden & Mack.
ATTORNEYS

INVENTOR
JACQUES YVES COUSTEAU,
BY Stone, Boyden & Mack.
ATTORNEYS

This patent for Jacques Cousteau's Diving Apparatus shows the original sketches for his invention.

no longer breathe. Diving would be impossible. The two men went back to lab for more work. They looked at the design. They moved some of the pieces around. Then Cousteau tested the gear in a water tank. It worked fine in the small tank. Would it also work in a big ocean?

Emile Gagnan and Jacques Cousteau applied for a patent. They called their new invention an Aqua-Lung. Cousteau went back to his ship. Gagnan built the first official Aqua-Lung. It was now time for the big test! Gagnan shipped the wooden box to Cousteau.

Will the Aqua-Lung Work?

Inside the box were three tanks of compressed air and an air regulator. There were two tubes coming out of the regulator. They connected to a mouthpiece. There was a harness to hold the tanks in place on the diver's back. The box also had a face mask and rubber foot fins. Jacques and Simone Cousteau, along with Tailliez and Dumas, went to the beach. They couldn't wait for Jacques to try the new Aqua-Lung.

The men helped Cousteau put on the gear. He splashed into the water and tried to go under. The air in the tanks made him float. Dumas put a belt on Cousteau. When weights were added to the belt, Cousteau sank. He tried breathing with the Aqua-Lung for the first time. Breathe in. Breathe out. Breathe in. Breathe out. It seemed to be working fine. He swam out into the cove underwater. Simone swam on top of the water. She wore a snorkel and goggles. She watched Jacques from above.

Cousteau swam down to 30 feet. He didn't feel pressure in his lungs. The Aqua-Lung was sending him just the right amount of air. He went a little deeper.

Jacques Cousteau swims with his Aqua-Lung.

His breathing was still easy and regular. When he got to the sandy bottom, he looked up. There on the surface was Simone. She watched Jacques through her goggles. He waved at her and she waved back.

Joy!

On that magical day, Cousteau rolled in the water. He stood upside down on one finger. Through it all, the Aqua-Lung did just what it was supposed to do. Cousteau swam into a little cave. He turned over on his back. The roof of the cave was covered with lobsters. He pulled two free and swam up to Simone. He handed the lobsters to her and went back for more. A lobster dinner would be a nice treat.

Cousteau finally came out of the water. "Back on shore we danced for joy," he said. That day changed everything for divers. They no longer would have to wear big diving suits. Hoses would not tie them to the surface. Instead they could swim and dive with the fish. During that first summer, the team made 500 dives.

real fact!

The Bends

Cousteau and his team were worried about getting an attack of the bends if they went any deeper than 132 feet. Why does this happen? The normal air we breathe is 78 percent nitrogen gas. We breathe it out when we exhale. Deep underwater, the nitrogen does not pass out of the body. It goes into the blood instead. Sometimes a diver rises too fast in the water. Then the nitrogen in the blood turns to little bubbles. The bubbles cause pain. Pain makes the body bend in strange ways. This is where the name "bends" comes from.

Divers come up slowly to keep from getting the bends.

Cousteau wanted to show others what he saw in the water. He built a waterproof case for his camera. He filmed as he swam. The divers gradually went deeper and deeper. They stopped when they reached 22 fathoms, which is 132 feet.

Jacques and Simone Cousteau

Calypso

The sea was where Jacques Cousteau wanted to be. He retired from the Navy and leased a ship in 1950. The *Calypso* was 150 feet long. It was fitted with a laboratory and film studio. It even had a helicopter landing pad. Jacques and Simone lived aboard the *Calypso*. Their sons went to boarding school. During summers and vacations, they lived on the ship too.

The *Calypso* sailed the oceans of the world. In 1953, Jacques Cousteau wrote a book, *The Silent World*. It was full of pictures and facts about the sea. The book was a bestseller that sold 5 million copies. Nobody had ever explored so much under the water before. People wanted to know more about the sea and the creatures in it.

The *Calypso* became home for Cousteau and his family. Here the ship spends some time near Antarctica.

Cousteau's son Philippe (right) co-starred in the television series.

Thousands of people also learned to dive. The name Aqua-Lung was replaced by the word SCUBA. SCUBA stands for Self-Contained Underwater Breathing Apparatus. The sport of SCUBA diving became very popular. Many people took it up as a hobby. They were able to view the undersea world.

Captain Cousteau

In 1968, a new show started on television. It was called *The Undersea World of Jacques Cousteau*. The one-hour specials ran for eight years. For the first time ever, people got to see amazing films from under the sea. Philippe co-starred with his famous father in the series.

People couldn't wait for the next episode. They saw hammerhead sharks and moray eels up close. Coral reefs with all of their bright colors lit up the TV screen. And always there was Captain Cousteau in his red cap. His gentle voice and French accent were the hit of television for many seasons.

While sailing the world, Jacques Cousteau noticed more and more pollution. The oceans had floating islands of trash and oil and dead fish. Captain Cousteau was very worried about the state of the world's water. He founded the Cousteau Society to raise money for ocean research.

Jacques Cousteau wears
his famous red cap.

Une prodigieuse révélation...

LE MONDE DU SILENCE

UN GRAND FILM EN EASTMANCOLOR
DE J.Y. COUSTEAU ET LOUIS MALLE
AVEC FREDERIC DUMAS, ALBERT FALCO LES PLONGEURS
ET L'EQUIPAGE DE LA CALYPSO

Jacques Cousteau codirected *Le Monde du Silence* (which means "The Silent World"). He shot the film from the *Calypso*. The documentary was one of the first to use underwater cameras to show deep ocean life.

He Made Diving Fun for All

Jacques Cousteau wrote dozens of books about life in the sea. He made movies and television shows. He showed the world all of the wonderful things that live in the oceans. Before the Aqua-Lung, only a few people were lucky enough to dive underwater. After his invention, millions of people got to see the wonderful world of the sea up close.

Captain Cousteau died in 1997 at the age of 87. He worked up until the time of his death. On the day when he first tested his Aqua-Lung, he said: "From this day forward we would swim across miles of country no man had known, free and level, with our flesh feeling what the fish scales know."

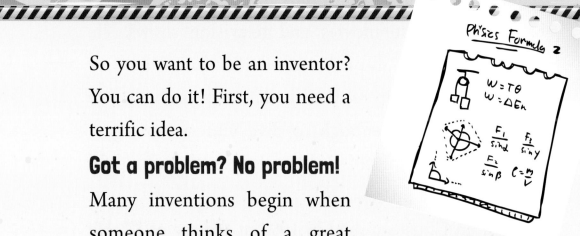

So you want to be an inventor? You can do it! First, you need a terrific idea.

Got a problem? No problem!

Many inventions begin when someone thinks of a great solution to a problem. One cold day in 1994, 10-year-old K.K. Gregory was building a snow fort. Soon, she had snow between her mittens and her coat sleeve. Her wrists were cold and wet. She found some scraps of fabric around the house, and used them to make a tube that would fit around her wrist. She cut a thumb hole in the tube to make a kind of fingerless glove, and called it a "Wristie." Wearing mittens over her new invention, her wrists stayed nice and warm when she played outside. Today, the Wristie business is booming.

Now it's your turn. Maybe, like K.K. Gregory, you have an idea for something new that would make your life better or easier. Perhaps you can think of a way to improve an everyday item. Twelve-year-old Becky Schroeder became one of the youngest people ever to receive a U.S. patent after she invented a glow-in-the-dark clipboard that allowed people to write in the dark. Do you like to play sports or board games? James Naismith, inspired by a game he used to play as a boy, invented a new game he called basketball.

Let your imagination run wild. You never know where it will take you.

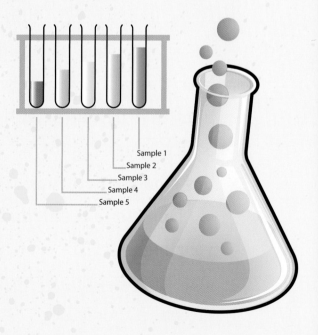

Sample 1
Sample 2
Sample 3
Sample 4
Sample 5

Research It!

Okay, you have a terrific idea for an invention. Now what do you do?

First, you'll want to make sure that nobody else has

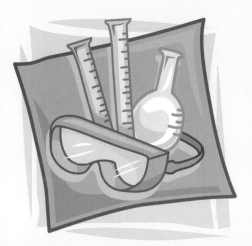

thought of your idea. You wouldn't want to spend hours developing your new invention, only to find that someone else beat you to it. Check out Google Patents (see Learn More for the website address), which can help you find out whether your idea is original.

Bring It to Life!

If no one else has thought of your idea, congratulations! Write it down in a notebook. Date and initial every entry you make. If you file a patent for your invention later, this will help you prove that you were the first to think of it. The most important thing about this logbook is that pages cannot be added or subtracted. You can buy a bound notebook at any office supply store.

Draw several different pictures of your invention in your logbook. Try sketching views from above, below, and to the side. Show how big each part of your invention should be.

Build a model. Don't be discouraged if it doesn't work at first. You may have to experiment with different designs and materials. That's part of the fun! Take pictures of everything, and tape them into your logbook. Try your invention out on your friends and family. If they have any suggestions to make it better, build another model. Perfect your invention, and give it a clever name.

Patent It!

Do you want to sell your invention? You'll want to apply for a patent. Holding a patent to your invention means that no one else can make, use, or sell your invention in the U.S. without your permission. It prevents 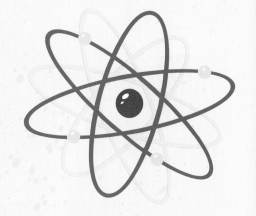 others from making money off your idea. You will definitely need an adult to help you apply for a patent. It can be a complicated and expensive process. But if you think that people will want to buy your invention, it is well worth it. Good luck!

TIMELINE

1910 Jacques–Yves Cousteau born in France on June 11.

1930 Entered French Naval Academy.

1937 Married Simone Melchoir.

1938 Son Jean–Michel born on May 6.

1940 Son Philippe born on December 30.

1943 Invented the Aqua–Lung with Emile Gagnan.

1950 Leased the ship *Calypso*.

1953 Published *The Silent World*.

1968–1976 Produced *The Undersea World of Jacques Cousteau* for television.

1973 Began Cousteau Society to explore and protect the world's oceans.

1979 Son Philippe died in an airplane crash.

1985 Awarded the Presidential Medal of Freedom.

1990 Wife Simone died.

1997 Jacques Cousteau died on June 25.

WORDS TO KNOW

compressed—To be squeezed into a smaller space.

exhale—To breathe out.

fathom—A unit used to measure water depth. One fathom equals six feet.

nitrogen—A colorless, odorless gas we breathe.

oxygen—A colorless, odorless gas we breathe.

patent—The legal right to be the only one to make an invention.

pressure—A force pressing down on something.

regulator—A device that controls the amount of pressure.

snorkel—A tube that a swimmer breathes through while face down in the water.

valve—A device that controls the flow of liquid or gas through a hose or pipe.

Books

Berne, Jennifer. *Manfish*. San Francisco, Calif.: Chronicle Books, 2008.

Hopping. Lorraine Jean. *Jacques Cousteau: Saving Our Seas*. New York: MacGraw-Hill Publishing Company, 2000.

Teitelbaum, Michael. *Scuba Diving*. Mankato, Minn.: Child's World, 2012.

Yaccarino, Dan. *The Fantastic Undersea Life of Jacques Cousteau*. New York: Dragonfly Books, 2012.

Internet Addresses

Cousteau Society. Cousteau Kids. 2013.
   <http://www.cousteau.org/cousteau-kids/
     cousteau-kids>

Google Patents.
   <http://google.com/patents>

INDEX